science for a changing world

Prepared in cooperation with the Bureau of Land Management

Assessment of Mercury and Methylmercury in Water, Sediment, and Biota in Sulphur Creek in the vicinity of the Clyde Gold Mine and the Elgin Mercury Mine, Colusa County, California

By Roger L. Hothem, James J. Rytuba, Brianne E. Brussee, and Daniel N. Goldstein

Open-File Report 2013-1056

U.S. Department of the Interior
U.S. Geological Survey

U.S. Department of the Interior
KEN SALAZAR, Secretary

U.S. Geological Survey
Suzette M. Kimball, Acting Director

U.S. Geological Survey, Reston, Virginia: 2013

For more information on the USGS—the Federal source for science about the Earth, its
natural and living resources, natural hazards, and the environment, visit *http://www.usgs.gov*
or call 1-888-ASK-USGS.

For an overview of USGS information products, including maps, imagery, and publications,
visit *http://www.usgs.gov/pubprod*

To order this and other USGS information products, visit *http://store.usgs.gov*

Suggested citation:
Hothem, R.L., Rytuba, J.J., Brussee, B.E., and Goldstein, D.N., 2013, Assessment of
mercury and methylmercury in water, sediment, and biota in Sulphur Creek in the vicinity of
the Clyde Gold Mine and the Elgin Mercury Mine, Colusa County, California: U.S. Geological
Survey Open-File Report 2013-1056, 38 p. [http://pubs.usgs.gov/of/2013/1056/]

Contents

Figures

Tables

Conversion Factors , Datum, and Abbreviations and Definitions

Conversion Factors

Multiply	By	To obtain
Length		
inch (in)	2.54	centimeter (cm)
inch (in)	25.4	millimeter (mm)
foot (ft)	0.3048	meter (m)
mile (mi)	1.609	kilometer (km)
acre	4,047	square meter (m^2)
acre	0.4047	hectare (ha)
acre	0.004047	square kilometer (km^2)
Volume		
gallon (gal)	3.785	liter (L)
gallon (gal)	0.003785	cubic meter (m^3)
cubic inch (in^3)	16.39	cubic centimeter (cm^3)
cubic inch (in^3)	0.01639	liter (L)
cubic foot (ft^3)	0.02832	cubic meter (m^3)
Flow rate		
cubic foot per second (ft^3/s)	0.02832	cubic meter per second (m^3/s)
gallon per minute (gal/min)	0.06309	liter per second (L/s)
Mass		
gram (g)	0.03527	ounce, avoirdupois (oz)
kilogram	2.205	pound, avoirdupois (lb)
microgram (μg)	0.0000000353	ounce, avoirdupois (oz)
milligram (mg)	0.0000353	ounce, avoirdupois (oz)
nanogram (ng)	0.0000000000353	ounce, avoirdupois (oz)
ounce, avoirdupois (oz)	28.35	gram (g)
pound, avoirdupois (lb)	0.4536	kilogram (kg)

Temperature in degrees Celsius (°C) may be converted to degrees Fahrenheit (°F) as follows:
$$°F = (1.8 \times °C) + 32$$
Temperature in degrees Fahrenheit (°F) may be converted to degrees Celsius (°C) as follows:
$$°C = (°F-32)/1.8$$

Concentrations of chemical constituents in water are given in milligrams per liter (mg/L, parts per million), micrograms per liter (μg/L, parts per billion), or nanograms per liter (ng/L, parts per trillion).

Concentrations of chemical constituents in tissues are given in micrograms per gram (μg/g, parts per million). Concentrations of chemical constituents in sediment are given in micrograms per gram (μg/g, parts per million) or nanograms per gram (ng/g, parts per billion)

Datum

Horizontal coordinate information is referenced to the North American Datum of 1983 (NAD 83).

Acronyms and Definitions

Au	gold
As	arsenic
Ba	barium
CDFG	California Department of Fish and Game
CERCLA	U.S. Environmental Protection Agency's Comprehensive Environmental Response, Compensation, and Liability Act
CVAFS	cold-vapor atomic-fluorescence spectroscopy
CVAAS	cold-vapor atomic-absorption spectroscopy
DOC	dissolved organic carbon
DOM	dissolved organic matter
Flask	34.5 kg or 76 lb of Hg
GC	gas chromatographic
GMWL	Global Meteoric Water Line
HCl	hydrochloric acid
HDPE	high-density polyethylene
H_2SO_4	sulfuric acid
Hg	Mercury; does not denote speciation
Hg_F	total mercury (inorganic plus organic) in a filtered sample (either 0.1 or 0.45 μm, as specified in the text)
Hg_T	total mercury (inorganic plus organic)
ICP-AES	inductively-coupled plasma atomic-emission spectroscopy
ICP-MS	inductively-coupled plasma-mass spectroscopy
KOH	potassium hydroxide
MDL	mean detection limit
MMeHg	monomethyl mercury, methylmercury, and monomethylmercury ion (CH_3Hg^+)
Na	sodium
ng/g	nanogram per gram, equivalent to parts per billion
NIST	National Institute of Standards and Technology
ng/L	nanogram per liter, equivalent to parts per trillion
ORP	oxidation-reduction potential
ppm	parts per million, equivalent to mg/kg or μg/g
QA/QC	quality assurance/quality control
Rb	rubidium
RPD	relative percent difference
RSI	Removal Site Investigation
Sb	antimony
SC	specific (electrical) conductivity, reported in units of millisiemens per centimeter (mS/cm) or microsiemens per centimeter (μS/cm) at 25 °C
SOP	standard operating procedure

Sr	strontium
TI	thallium
USBLM	U.S. Bureau of Land Management
USEPA	U.S. Environmental Protection Agency
USGS	U.S. Geological Survey
W	tungsten
ww	wet weight

Acknowledgments

This field investigation was funded by the Bureau of Land Management. The California Department of Fish and Game granted permission to collect specimens for this study.

W. Perry of the Dixon Field Station, USGS, prepared the map. We appreciate the excellent reviews of earlier versions of this report by J. Fleck, J. May, and T. Kimball.

Assessment of Mercury and Methylmercury in Water, Sediment, and Biota in Sulphur Creek in the vicinity of the Clyde Gold Mine and the Elgin Mercury Mine, Colusa County, California

By Roger L. Hothem,[1] James J. Rytuba,[2] Brianne E. Brussee,[1] and Daniel N. Goldstein[2]

Abstract

At the request of the U.S. Bureau of Land Management, we performed a study during April–July 2010 to characterize mercury (Hg), monomethyl mercury (MMeHg), and other geochemical constituents in sediment, water, and biota at the Clyde Gold Mine and the Elgin Mercury Mine, located in neighboring subwatersheds of Sulphur Creek, Colusa County, California. This study was in support of a Comprehensive Environmental Response, Compensation, and Liability Act - Removal Site Investigation. The investigation was in response to an abatement notification from the California Central Valley Regional Water Quality Control Board to evaluate the release of Hg from the Clyde and Elgin mines. Samples of water, sediment, and biota (aquatic macroinvertebrates) were collected from sites upstream and downstream from the two mine sites to evaluate the level of Hg contamination contributed by each mine to the aquatic ecosystem. Physical parameters, as well as dissolved organic carbon, total Hg (Hg_T), and MMeHg were analyzed in water and sediment. Other relevant geochemical constituents were analyzed in sediment, filtered water, and unfiltered water. Samples of aquatic macroinvertebrates from each mine were analyzed for Hg_T and MMeHg. The presence of low to moderate concentrations of Hg_T and MMeHg in water, sediment, and biota from the Freshwater Branch of Sulphur Creek, and the lack of significant increases in these concentrations downstream from the Clyde Mine indicated that this mine is not a significant source of Hg to the watershed during low flow conditions. Although concentrations of Hg_T and MMeHg were generally higher in samples of sediment and water from the Elgin Mine compared to the Clyde Mine, concentrations in comparable biota from the two mine areas were similar. It is likely that highly saline effluent from nearby hot springs contribute more Hg to the West Fork of Sulphur Creek than the mine waste material at the Elgin Mine.

---

[1]U.S. Geological Survey, Dixon, California.

[2]U.S. Geological Survey, Menlo Park, California.

Introduction

The U.S. Bureau of Land Management (USBLM) received an abatement notification from the Central Valley Regional Water Quality Control Board to address release of mercury (Hg) from the Clyde Gold Mine and the Elgin Mercury Mine. In response, the USBLM requested that the U.S. Geological Survey (USGS) measure and characterize Hg and other geochemical constituents in sediment, water, and biota at the Clyde and Elgin mines in support of a Comprehensive Environmental Response, Compensation, and Liability Act (CERCLA) - Removal Site Investigation (RSI). The RSI applies to removal of Hg-contaminated mine waste from the Elgin and Clyde mines, as well as nearby Harley Gulch. Because the two mines, located in adjacent subwatersheds in the headwaters of Sulphur Creek, are within the California Coast Range mercury mineral belt (Rytuba, 2000), it is likely that Hg contamination could originate from both naturally occurring and anthropogenic sources.

The Clyde Gold Mine is a small, relatively low production mine about 6 km northwest of Wilbur Springs on land managed by the USBLM in the headwaters of the Sulphur Creek Watershed, Colusa County, California (fig. 1). Gold (Au) was discovered near the Clyde Mine in the 1860s, mine workings were constructed in the 1880s, and mining continued sporadically until 1890. The Clyde Mine reportedly produced about "$200 per day" of Au in the late 1880s, but it was abandoned by 1890 when prohibitive amounts of groundwater were encountered (Watts, 1893). Ore was processed on-site with a 3.5-foot Huntington mill until 1890, at which point a 5-foot Huntington mill was installed to process ore. A trommel-type Au recovery system was installed in the 1970s, presumably to reprocess old waste material on-site. This trommel system is believed to have caused the tailings pile and small ponds visible on-site today. The on-site processing of Au ore produced waste material that could have contributed Hg to Freshwater Branch, a small creek that flows through the mine site. Workings at the Clyde Mine include three partially open adits containing standing water, several cuts and trenches to the west and southeast of the adits, and a stormwater retention pond southeast of the adits.

The mineralized area at the Clyde Mine is hosted within serpentinite and shales of the Great Valley Sequence in the west part of the mine area. The Au mineralizes in fracture zones in a northwest-southeast trending, silicified body of serpentinite. Native Au and pyrite are reportedly found at the mine site in decomposed soft slate and shale.

The Elgin Mercury Mine is about 1.6 km south of the Clyde Mine and about 4.75 km northwest of Wilbur Springs on West Fork of Sulphur Creek, Colusa County, California (fig. 1). Part of the mine is on land managed by the USBLM. Mercury was discovered near the Elgin Mine in the 1870s, and at least 52 flasks (about 1,800 kg) of Hg were produced in 1875 (Mining and Scientific Press, 1875). Ore assaying about 1.8 percent Hg was mined intermittently until 1916 (Huguenin, 1917). The high temperature water and rock present in the area prohibited further exploration and mining. Compared to other Hg mines in the area, total production at the Elgin Mine was minimal. The nearby Abbott-Turkey Run Mine produced over 50,000 flasks of Hg from 1862 to 1971 (U.S. Bureau of Mines, 1965).

Workings include three adits, 500 feet of underground workings that have since collapsed, and two areas containing significant surface disruption (Tetra Tech, 2003). Ore was processed with a 10-pipe retort equipped with a furnace and Griffin mill to concentrate cinnabar (HgS), the principal ore mineral. Waste-rock piles exist around the open cuts, with an estimated total volume of 1,000-4,000 cubic yards (Churchill and Clinkenbeard, 2003). A small tailings pile is present on the west side of West Fork of Sulphur Creek.

The country rock in the Elgin Mine region comprises serpentinite and shale of the Great Valley Sequence. The principal Hg mineralization product, cinnabar, is primarily found where serpentinite is in fault contact with shale. Cinnabar is concentrated in fracture zones in silicified serpentinite and locally leached by acidic fluids in the near surface (Tetra Tech, 2003).

This report summarizes data obtained from field sampling in the Sulphur Creek Watershed near the Clyde and Elgin mine areas that took place in 2010 to provide an assessment of Hg and related chemical constituents in water, sediment, and biota in the study area.

Methods

Sample Locations

Clyde Mine

Samples were collected to assess the concentration of Hg and biogeochemically relevant constituents affecting Hg transport and methylation of Hg in Freshwater Branch, a stream that runs next to the Clyde Mine and is a tributary to the East Fork of Sulphur Creek (fig. 1, table 1). Water, sediment, and biota were sampled from Freshwater Branch, upstream and downstream from the mine workings, to characterize the amount of Hg contributed to the watershed by waste material from the Clyde Mine during low-flow conditions (fig. 1, table 1). Sites sampled for biota were centered approximately on the locations listed in table 1, but sampling normally included as much as 50 meters (m) of stream. Unless otherwise specified, biota sites overlapped sites sampled for water and sediment. Sample sites 10CL1 (water and sediment, fig. 2) and CLUS (biota) were upstream from the mine workings in Freshwater Branch (fig. 1). Water and sediment site 10CL2 (fig. 3) was about 130 m upstream from the corresponding biota site (CLMN), but both were in Freshwater Branch downstream from the mine-waste piles (fig. 1). Site 10CL3 (water and sediment) was about 330 m downstream from biota site CLDS (fig. 4), but both were in similar habitats on the Freshwater Branch downstream from the Clyde Mine. Site 10CL4 (water and sediment) and CLOK (biota, fig. 5) were in Oak Cove, a small tributary to Freshwater Branch downstream from the other sample sites (fig. 1).

Elgin Mine

Samples for water, sediment, and biota were collected at four locations in the Elgin Mine area (fig. 1, table 1). Three of the sites were on the West Fork of Sulphur Creek, which flows adjacent to the Elgin Mine. Sites 10EL1 (water and sediment) and ESUS (biota, fig. 6) were near one another upstream from the confluence of West Fork Sulphur Creek and Salt Branch (fig. 1), and 10EL2 (water and sediment) and ESDS (biota, fig. 7), were just downstream from that confluence. Site 10EL3 (fig. 8*A*), a water and sediment site, was about 400 m downstream from the corresponding biota site, EWSU (fig. 8*B*). One site, ESLT, on Salt Branch, about 975 m upstream from West Fork Sulphur Creek, was considered a reference site. Only biota was collected from ESLT (fig. 9).

Field Methods

Sediment

Wet sediment samples were collected from the streams and placed in 250 mL polycarbonate jars for analysis of monomethyl mercury (MMeHg) and total mercury (Hg_T). These samples were stored on wet ice in the field and shipped overnight on dry ice to the analytical laboratory where they were kept frozen until analysis. The temperature of samples arriving at the analytical facilities was $\leq -25°C$.

A dry sediment sample was collected in a Ziploc® bag for analysis of major and minor elements, stored at ambient temperature, and shipped to the analytical laboratory at ambient temperature without preservation. Replicate sediment samples were not collected for this study.

Water

Water variables, including pH, conductivity, temperature, dissolved oxygen, and oxidation-reduction potential (ORP) were measured in the field by placing the probe of a battery-powered Hydrolab Sonde directly into the flowing stream water (Gibs and others, 2007).

Water samples were then collected from the streams by using a peristaltic pump equipped with ultraclean tubing and an inline filter (0.45-μm pore size) for analysis of anions and alkalinity. During every sampling event, a field blank was collected by processing de-ionized water and performing the same analyses (except for alkalinity) following the same procedures as were used for the field samples. Samples for major- and minor-element determinations in filtered and unfiltered water samples were acidified to less than pH 2 with trace metal (Ultrex, J.T. Baker)-grade nitric acid (HNO_3) and stored in acid-washed, high-density polyethylene (HDPE) bottles. Subsamples for anion and alkalinity measurements were filtered, stored in HDPE bottles, and chilled to approximately 4°C until analysis, in accordance with USGS protocols for trace metals (U.S. Geological Survey, 2006).

Samples for Hg_T, total Hg in filtered water samples (Hg_F), and MMeHg analyses were collected in trace metal-free-certified 250-ml fluoropolymer bottles (Nalgene ICHEM) with no headspace. All samples were collected from the stream at the same time, but the Hg_F samples were filtered with a 0.45-micron filter. The MMeHg bottles contained a preservative of hydrochloric acid (HCl) provided by the analytical laboratory, Frontier Global Sciences (Seattle, Wash.). Procedures for Hg_T analysis followed ultra-clean sampling and handling protocols (Bloom, 1995; Gill and Fitzgerald, 1987) during the collection of field samples and analysis to avoid introduction of Hg. Samples were kept on ice until shipped. Samples were shipped on ice packs and arrived the next morning at the analytical facilities at temperatures ranging from 1 to 4° C, as specified by U.S. Environmental Protection Agency (EPA) Method 1631E to minimize biologically induced phase changes and MMeHg degradation (U.S. Environmental Protection Agency, 2002).

Biota

Aquatic invertebrates can serve as excellent indicators of metal contamination (bioindicators; for example, Cain and others, 1992). Predatory insects were the target macroinvertebrates (Merritt and Cummins, 1995) for this study, with primary taxa dependent on abundance and availability at sampling sites. Invertebrate taxa collected in 2010 from the Clyde Mine were adult water striders (order Hemiptera, family Gerridae), larval dragonflies (order Odonata, families Aeshnidae, Cordulegastridae, Gomphidae, and Libellulidae), and larval dobsonflies (order Megaloptera, family Corydalidae). Taxa collected from the Elgin Mine were larval damselflies (order Odonata, family Coenagrionidae), adult water striders, predaceous diving beetles (order Coleoptera, family Dytiscidae), larval water scavenger beetles (order Coleoptera, family Hydrophilidae), and larval dobsonflies.

Aquatic invertebrates were collected by using dip nets and by hand and placed in Ziploc® plastic bags with native water (Alpers and others, 2005). Samples were kept in a cooler and allowed to depurate in native water on wet ice for 4–24 hours before processing. Individuals were sorted by family and placed in disposable dishes by using Teflon™-coated forceps or by hand while wearing disposable latex gloves. Organisms were rinsed clean with deionized water, patted dry with a clean paper towel, and composited by family, with the goal of obtaining a minimum of 1 gram (g) wet biomass. Each invertebrate sample consisted of 1–23 individuals of the same family (0.38–3.57 g total mass). Samples were weighed on an electronic balance (± 0.01 g), placed into chemically cleaned glass jars (VWR TraceClean™) with Teflon-lined lids, and stored frozen until they were shipped on dry ice to the contract laboratory for analysis within 30 days after processing. The samples were analyzed for Hg_T and MMeHg at Frontier Global Sciences, Inc., in Seattle, Wash.

Analytical Methods

Sediment

Multi-element analyses for all dry-sediment samples were performed at ALS Chemex laboratories (Reno, Nev.). Bulk samples were ground in a zirconia ring mill and subjected to a near-total four-acid digestion. Major elements were determined by inductively coupled-atomic emission spectroscopy (ICP-AES). Minor elements, other than Hg, were determined by ICP–mass spectroscopy (ICP-MS). Mercury was determined by cold vapor atomic absorption spectroscopy (CVAAS) following methods similar to those described by Crock (1996) and O'Leary and others (1996).

Mercury and MMeHg analyses for all wet sediment were done at Frontier Global Sciences. For Hg_T, the sediment was leached with cold aqua regia, followed by stannous chloride ($SnCl_2$) reduction, two-stage Au amalgamation, and cold vapor atomic fluorescence spectroscopy (CVAFS) detection. MMeHg was obtained by acid bromide/methyl chloride extraction, followed by aqueous-phase ethylation, isothermal gas chromatographic (GC) separation, and CVAFS detection (Horvat and others, 1993). Results were reported on both a wet- and dry-weight basis.

Water

Analyses for anions and alkalinity were performed at the USGS laboratory in Denver, Colo. Anion (sulfate, chloride, nitrate, and fluoride) concentrations were determined by ion chromatography (Fishman and Pyen, 1979). Alkalinity as calcium carbonate ($CaCO_3$) was determined by using Gran's titration with sulfuric acid (H_2SO_4; Orion Research, Inc., 1978), within 2–4 days after sample collection.

Cations were determined by using ICP–AES and ICP–MS. The ICP-AES analyses were determined in USGS laboratories under the direction of Paul Briggs. Duplicate water samples, blank samples, and USGS Water Resource Division standard reference waters were analyzed with the data set.

Mercury analyses in surface waters were performed at Frontier Global Sciences Inc. (Seattle, Wash.). Samples were handled in a Class-100 clean-air station, and ultra-clean Hg trace-metal protocol was followed. Primary standards used in the laboratory were NIST-certified, or traceable to NIST-certified materials and calibrated against DORM-2 (National Research Council of Canada Institute for National Measurement Standards, 1999). USEPA Method 1631 was used (U.S. Environmental Protection Agency, 2002). Total Hg was determined by bromine monochloride (BrCl) oxidation followed by Tin(II) Chloride ($SnCl_2$) reduction, two-stage gold amalgamation, and detection by CVAFS (Bloom and others, 1988). MMeHg was liberated from water by using an all-Teflon® distillation system and analyzed by using aqueous phase ethylation with purging onto Carbotrap™, isothermal GC separation, and CVAFS detection (Bloom, 1989). Quality-assurance measures were employed with the following minimum frequencies: laboratory duplicates, one per ten samples; method blanks, three per analytical batch; filtration blanks, one per ten samples; and spike recovery or standard reference material, one per ten samples.

Biota

At Frontier Global Sciences, benthic samples were rinsed with reagent water and blotted with clean laboratory wipes prior to being homogenized. Homogenized samples were digested for Hg_T analysis with concentrated sulfuric and nitric acids according to Frontier Global Sciences' SOP FGS-011, a modification of USEPA method 1631. Total Hg in digested tissues was analyzed by $SnCl_2$ reduction, dual Au amalgamation, and CVAFS detection according to FGS-069, a modification of USEPA method 1631.

Homogenized samples were digested for MMeHg analysis by a heated 25 percent potassium hydroxide (KOH) solution, followed by dilution with methanol, according to FGS-010. MMeHg in digested tissues was analyzed by CV-GC-AFS (aqueous phase ethylation, isothermal GC separation, and CVAFS detection) according to Frontier Global Sciences' SOP FGS-070, a modified EPA 1630 procedure.

All results are presented on a wet-weight basis, but, where sufficient sample mass was available, percentage moisture is presented to allow for dry-weight calculations.

QA/QC

Sediment

Procedural blanks, matrix spiked (MS) samples, and laboratory control samples (LCS) were analyzed to assure the accuracy of the methods. To assure that no analyte was added during the processing of the sample, procedural blanks were analyzed at a rate of 5 percent of the total samples, with at least one per matrix per analytical run. In all blanks for Hg_T (n=3) and for MMeHg (n=3), the analyte was undetected, although included in the analysis. All blank results met the acceptable criterion of less than twice the mean detection limit (MDL; Hg_T = 0.36 ng/g; MMeHg = 0.008 ng/g).

Duplicate sediment samples were analyzed at a rate of 5 percent, with at least one duplicate per matrix per analytical run to estimate the precision of the methods. The relative percentage differences (RPDs) for Hg_T duplicates were 0.119 and 0.787, both less than the 25 percent acceptable criterion, but the RPDs for MMeHg duplicates were 4.73 and 136 percent. The one RPD exceeded the 25 percent criterion because the sample matrix was not homogeneous. However, the batch quality control was accepted on the basis of LCS/laboratory control sample duplicates (LCS/LCSD) RPD.

Matrix spikes and MS duplicates (MSDs) of Hg_T and MMeHg used to verify that the matrix characteristics did not interfere with the analytical results were analyzed at a rate of 5 percent, with at least one spike per matrix per analytical run. The Hg_T MS and MSD recoveries (n=4) ranged from 84.7 to 2,850 percent, only two of which were within the acceptable criteria of 75–125 percent. According to Frontier Global Sciences, the two recoveries were outside the acceptable limits because the spike concentration was less than two times the sample concentration; however, the batches were acceptable because LCS and LCSD recoveries were within control limits. The RPDs (n=2) were 13.3 and 180 percent. The one RPD exceeded the 25 percent criterion likely because the sample matrix was not homogeneous; however, the batch quality control was accepted on the basis of LCS/LCSD RPD.

The MMeHg MS and MSD recoveries (n=2) were 117 and 118 percent, both within the acceptable criteria (65–130 percent). The RPD was 0.872, well below the acceptable criterion of 25 percent.

LCS and LCSDs were analyzed at a rate of 5 percent to insure that the method worked with naturally incorporated Hg. Recoveries of Hg_T in LCS and LCSDs (n = 2) were 102 and 104 percent, well within the criterion of 75–125 percent. The LCS RPD for Hg_T was 1.69 percent, meeting the criterion of $\leq$ 25 percent. For MMeHg, LCS and LCSD recoveries (n = 2) were 72.4 and 76.4 percent, within the criterion of 70–130 percent. The LCS RPD was 5.39 percent, meeting the criterion of $\leq$ 25 percent.

Water

As with sediment, procedural blanks were analyzed for water at a rate of 5 percent of the total samples, with at least one per matrix per analytical run. In all blanks for Hg_T (n=10), and for MMeHg (n=6), the analyte was undetected, although included in the analysis. All blank results were less than the acceptable criteria of twice the MDL (Hg_T = 0.50 ng/L; MMeHg = 0.050 ng/L).

Duplicate water samples were analyzed at a rate of 5 percent, with at least one duplicate per matrix per analytical run to estimate the precision of the methods. The RPDs for Hg_T and MMeHg duplicates were all less than 25 percent, the acceptable criterion.

Matrix spike samples and MSDs of Hg_T and MMeHg were analyzed at a rate of 5 percent, with at least one spike per matrix per analytical run. The Hg_T MS and MSD recoveries (n=12) ranged from 84.5 to 116 percent, all within the acceptable criteria of 75–125 percent. The RPDs (n=6) ranged from 0.049 to 7.41 percent, all less than the acceptable criterion of 25 percent.

The MMeHg MS and MSD recoveries (n=4) ranged from 115 to 127 percent, all within the acceptable criteria of 65-130 percent. The RPDs (n=2) ranged from 2.59 to 10.4 percent, well below the acceptable criterion of 25 percent.

LCS and LCSDs were analyzed at a rate of 5 percent to insure that the method worked with naturally incorporated mercury. Recoveries of Hg_T in LCS and LCSDs (n = 8) ranged from 94.4 to 98.5 percent, well within the criterion of 80–120 percent. RPDs for Hg_T ranged from 0.074 to 1.00 percent, less than the 25 percent criterion. For MMeHg, LCS and LCSD recoveries (n = 4) ranged from 79.7 to 121 percent, within the criterion of 70–130 percent. LCS RPDs (n = 2), however, were 27.8 and 30.7 percent, both exceeding the acceptable limit of 25 percent. Frontier Global Sciences reported that the batch quality control was acceptable because the matrix duplicate and MS/MSD RPD values were within control limits.

Biota

As with sediment and water samples, procedural blanks were analyzed for biota at a rate of 5 percent of the total samples, with at least one per matrix per analytical run. No Hg_T (n=9) or MMeHg (n=12) was detected in any of the procedural blanks that were analyzed. All blank results were less than the acceptable criteria of twice the MDL (Hg_T = 0.142 ng/g; MMeHg = 0.40 ng/g).

Duplicate biota samples were analyzed at a rate of 5 percent, with at least one duplicate per matrix per analytical run to estimate the precision of the methods. The RPDs for two of the Hg_T duplicates (6.92–18.5 percent) were less than the acceptance criterion (25 percent), but the RPD for the third duplicate, 38.4 percent, exceeded the acceptable criterion. Nevertheless, the quality control for this analytical run was acceptable because MSD and LCS/LCSD RPD values were within control limits. The RPDs for two of the MMeHg sample duplicates (12.0 and 20.9 percent) were less than the acceptance criterion (25 percent), but the RPD for the third duplicate, 25.5 percent, barely exceeded the acceptable criterion.

MS and MSDs of Hg_T and MMeHg were analyzed at a rate of 5 percent, with at least one spike per matrix per analytical run. Spikes were samples fortified with a known quantity of analyte and analyzed as part of the run. The Hg_T MS and MSD recoveries (n=6) ranged from 81.3 to 119 percent, all within the acceptable criteria of 75–125 percent. The RPDs (n=3) ranged from 19.4 to 31.4 percent, one falling outside the acceptable criterion of less than 25 percent. Although the one RPD was outside of acceptance limits, the analytical-run quality control was deemed acceptable on the basis of MSD or LCS/LCSD RPD values, or both, that were within control limits.

The MMeHg MS and MSD recoveries (n=12) ranged from 46.0 to 249 percent, and all but three were within the acceptable criteria of 65–135 percent. The RPDs (n=5) ranged from 4.27 to 80.8 percent, with two greater than the acceptable criterion of 25 percent. However, these two recoveries were outside the acceptable limits because the spike concentration was less than twice the sample concentration. The third recovery (249 percent) and its RPD (80.8 percent) were greater than the acceptable limits because of a lack of sample homogeneity. All analytical runs were accepted, however, on the basis of LCS/LCSD recoveries that were within control limits and, when analysis permitted, acceptable analytical samples and analytical sample duplicates (AS/ASD).

LCS and LCSDs were analyzed at a rate of 5 percent to insure that the method worked with naturally incorporated mercury. Recoveries of Hg_T in LCS and LCSDs (n = 4) ranged from 95.9 to 100 percent, well within the criterion of 75 to 125 percent. RPDs for Hg_T were 0.246 and 0.413 percent, below the criterion of 25 percent. For MMeHg, LCS and LCSD recoveries (n = 5) ranged from 81.4 to 128 percent, within the criterion of 70 to 130 percent. LCS RPDs (n = 3) ranged from 0.573 to 5.92 percent, less than the criterion of 25 percent.

The ratio of Hg_T to MMeHg in biological samples ranged from 43.4 to 126.8 percent at the Clyde Mine and from 8.8 to 171.2 percent at the Elgin Mine. The percentage of MMeHg in these samples exceeded 100 percent in 8 of 18 samples at the Clyde Mine and in 4 of 11 samples at the Elgin Mine. However, we considered only those that were greater than 120 percent MMeHg to be problematic: two at Elgin Mine and three at Clyde Mine. According to Bloom (1992), nearly all of this variability can be explained by the analytical variability of Hg_T and MMeHg. Poorly homogenized samples showed greater variability, primarily because Hg_T and MMeHg are measured on separate aliquots, which vary in Hg concentration, not speciation. We considered the results of the analyses of MMeHg in biota, the biologically incorporated form of Hg, to be the more reliable than Hg_T for the purposes of this report.

Results

Mercury and Monomethyl Mercury in Sediment

Clyde Mine

Sediment in the Freshwater Branch upstream from the Clyde Mine waste piles (site 10CL1, fig. 2) did not have elevated Hg_T concentrations (259 nanograms per gram [ng/g]; table 2) compared to local background levels. Immediately downstream from the mine waste piles at sample site 10CL2 (fig. 3), Hg_T levels were lower (188 ng/g) than the upstream site, indicating that Hg was not being released in bulk sediment from the mine wastes into the creek during the sampling period. Further downstream from the mine workings at sample site 10CL3, the Hg_T concentration was higher (352 ng/g) than the most upstream site. At the sample site in the Oak Cove tributary to Freshwater Branch (10CL4), the Hg_T concentration in sediment was the lowest, at 109 ng/g. The concentration observed at sample site 10CL4 was representative of background in this watershed. The low concentrations of Hg_T (table 2) and other trace metals (table 3) in the sediment indicated that Hg-bearing sediment was not present in the stream reach near the Clyde Mine during low-flow conditions encountered at the time of sampling.

MMeHg concentrations in sediment sampled from the Freshwater Branch were not significantly elevated, and their pattern was generally similar to the concentration of Hg in the sediment at the four sample sites (table 2). At sample site 10CL1, upstream from the mine tailings, the MMeHg concentration was 0.49 ng/g. Just below the mine wastes at site 10CL2, the MMeHg concentration was lower (0.07 ng/g). The MMeHg concentration increased at sample site 10CL3, but only moderately to 0.52 ng/g. The concentration of MMeHg at sample site 10CL4 (0.15 ng/g) was near background levels.

The percentage MMeHg in sediment (table 2) was indicative of the net MMeHg production on a site-specific basis when the concentration of MMeHg was normalized to the total concentration of Hg (Drott and others, 2008). The percentage MMeHg was derived by dividing the measured concentrations of MMeHg by the measured concentrations of Hg in sediment at the same site:

Percentage of MMeHg = [(MMeHg in sediment, ng/g)/(Hg total in sediment, ng/g)]*100

The percentage of MMeHg levels in samples near the Clyde Mine were relatively constant and low, averaging from 0.19 percent upstream from the tailings input at site 10CL1 and varying slightly to 0.04 percent at site 10CL2, 0.15 percent at site 10CL3, and 0.14 percent at site 10CL4 (table 2). These low values indicated that limited MMeHg was being produced in the Freshwater Branch of Sulphur Creek at the time of sampling.

Elgin Mine

Sediment in the West Fork upstream from the main tailings piles at the Elgin Mine (site 10EL3) contained elevated Hg_T concentrations (2,800 ng/g; see table 2). Immediately downstream from the tailings piles, at sample site 10EL1, Hg_T concentrations were significantly higher at 16,400 ng/g. Furthest downstream from the mine area, at sample site 10EL2, Hg_T concentrations were the lowest observed locally, at 761 ng/g. The West Fork of Sulphur Creek receives uncontaminated water and sediment from Salt Fork, upstream from sample site 10EL2, which likely dilutes Hg_T in sediment at this site. These levels of Hg_T in sediment indicated that the tailings piles at the Elgin Mine were contributing significant amounts of Hg_T -enriched sediment to the West Fork of Sulphur Creek at the time of sampling.

MMeHg concentrations in West Fork sediment were moderate and showed a trend similar to Hg_T, with highest concentrations just downstream from the mine and lowest concentrations furthest downstream (table 2). Upstream from the mine tailings (10EL3), MMeHg levels were moderate, at 0.97 ng/g, but below the mine tailings piles, at site 10EL1, MMeHg levels (4.04 ng/g) were four times higher. As observed for Hg_T, the MMeHg concentration was lowest at the most downstream site (0.67 ng/g).

The percentage of MMeHg levels were relatively constant and low in samples collected from the West Fork, at 0.03 percent both upstream from the tailings input at site 10EL3 and at sample site 10EL1, and 0.09 percent at site 10EL2. These low values demonstrated that MMeHg production was limited in the West Fork of Sulphur Creek during the time of sampling.

Water Chemistry

Clyde Mine

The water in the Freshwater Branch of Sulphur Creek was slightly alkaline to neutral, with pH ranging from 7.37 to 7.89 (table 2). The water had low conductivity, ranging from 730 to 998 microsiemens per centimeter (μS/cm). Sulfate levels were slightly elevated, 11.4–23.0 parts per million (ppm), and carbonate concentrations were high, ranging from 416.5 to 583.5 ppm (table 5). Dissolved organic carbon (DOC) levels were relatively low in the Freshwater Branch compared to the West Fork (table 2). Oxygen and deuterium stable-isotope levels plotted near the Global Meteoric Water Line (GMWL), indicating that the water in the Freshwater Branch of Sulphur Creek was predominantly meteoric, with some evaporation causing the minor shift away from the GMWL (fig. 10). Concentrations of metals typically associated with Au deposits, such as As, Sb, Tl, and W, were all present at low levels in both filtered (table 6) and unfiltered (table 7) water samples from all four samples sites.

Elgin Mine

The water in the West Fork of Sulphur Creek was slightly alkaline, ranging in pH from 7.57 to 8.56 (table 2). The water was highly saline, with conductivity ranging from 23,097 to 25,899 μS/cm. Sulfate levels were elevated, ranging from 439 to 469 ppm, and carbonate concentrations were high, ranging from 2,765 to 3,380 ppm (table 5). Oxygen and deuterium stable-isotope levels plotted off the GMWL (fig. 10), indicating that the creek water was composed primarily of effluent from the numerous hot springs present in the area of the Elgin Mine. Slightly elevated levels of As, Ba, Na, Rb, Sr, and W were measured in the West Fork of Sulphur Creek (tables 8 and 9).

Mercury and Monomethyl Mercury in Water

Clyde Mine

The Hg_T levels in water in the Freshwater Branch of Sulphur Creek were low compared to other mine areas, with only one sample (10CL1) exceeding 50 nanograms per liter (ng/L) and the rest less than or equal to 16.0 ng/L (table 2). At sample site 10CL1, upstream from the mine tailings, the concentration of Hg_T was 16 ng/L, while the Hg_F was 9.45 ng/L. Just downstream from the Clyde Mine tailings (site 10CL2), Hg_T levels were relatively high (76.1 ng/L), but Hg_F (7.81 ng/L) was comparable to the upstream site. Further downstream from the mine at site 10CL3, Hg_T, and Hg_F declined to very low levels (3.45 and 3.14, respectively), similar to that found at the Oak Cove site (10CL4; table 2). The low values downstream demonstrated that much of the particulate Hg in upstream waters was not transported to the downstream site during the flow conditions in which we sampled. The relatively higher levels of total and dissolved Hg_T in the mine area could reflect Hg introduced into the mineralized area during formation of the Au deposit, or could represent Hg introduced to the system during amalgamation in gold recovery. The lack of specific mining records precludes definitive identification of the Hg source.

Elgin Mine

The Hg levels in all filtered and unfiltered water samples from the West Fork of Sulphur Creek were elevated (table 2). At sample site 10EL3, upstream from the main mine tailings, water had concentrations of 1,450 ng/L of Hg_T and 305 ng/L of Hg_F. Downstream from the mine area at site 10EL1, Hg_T increased to 1,580 ng/L and Hg_F increased to 394 ng/L. At the sample site furthest downstream from the mine, 10EL2, levels decreased to 1,200 ng/L Hg_T and 362 ng/L Hg_F. The high Hg concentrations in unfiltered water downstream from the mine indicated that Hg was being transported into the West Fork of Sulphur Creek from the Elgin Mine during the period of sampling. However, high concentrations of Hg_F indicated that the geothermal, saline spring source of water to Sulphur Creek in this area could contribute significant amounts of naturally occurring Hg to the system.

Mercury and Monomethyl Mercury in Biota

Clyde Mine

Concentrations of MMeHg and Hg_T in the invertebrates collected from the area of the Clyde Mine were far lower than concentrations documented at nearby Harley Gulch in 2002 (Rytuba and others, 2011). Concentrations in Clyde Mine invertebrates, however, were similar to those in comparable taxa from Harley Gulch after the remediation of the Abbott and Turkey Run Mines in 2010 and 2011. Water striders (Gerridae) had similar MMeHg concentrations at the three Freshwater Branch sampling sites (table 10). Larval dragonflies were collected from all four sampling sites in the Clyde Mine area, and MMeHg concentrations in two dragonfly families, Gomphidae and Aeshnidae, were not different among sites (fig. 11). Dobsonfly larvae collected from the site in Freshwater Branch farthest downstream from the mine (CLDS) were the exception, with five times more MMeHg (0.32 µg/g) than dobsonflies from the Oak Cove reference site (CLOK: 0.06 µg/g; table 10). As expected, the invertebrates collected from CLOK had MMeHg concentrations that were lower than, or similar to, the same taxa collected from the Freshwater Branch sites. With the exception of the CLDS dobsonflies, there were no apparent trends in concentrations of MMeHg or Hg_T in any taxon of aquatic invertebrate from Freshwater Branch.

Elgin Mine

Wide ranges of concentrations of Hg_T (0.01–1.62 µg/g) and MMeHg (0.01–1.90 µg/g) were present in invertebrate samples collected from the Elgin Mine area (table 10, fig. 12). The trend was for lower concentrations of both Hg_T and MMeHg at the site above the Elgin Mine (EWSU) and at the reference site (ESLT), with higher concentrations at the two sites below the Elgin Mine, ESUS and ESDS. The exception was water striders (Gerridae) which had a moderate concentration of MMeHg (0.12 µg/g) at EWSU, the site upstream from the mine, compared with lower concentrations just downstream from the mine (ESUS: 0.07 µg/g) and downstream from the confluence with Salt Branch (ESDS: 0.07 µg/g). Water striders were not collected from the reference site (ESLT).

MMeHg concentrations in both predaceous diving beetles (0.059 µg/g) and Dobsonflies (0.006 µg/g) collected from ESLT were the lowest found in the Elgin Mine area, indicating the site was suitable for use as a reference. The concentration of MMeHg in beetles from ESLT was about half that found at the Harley Gulch reference site in 2011 (Rytuba and others, 2011), while the concentration of MMeHg in dobsonfly larvae at ESLT was about one-fourth that found at the Harley Gulch reference in 2008 (Rytuba and others, 2011). The mean concentration of MMeHg in 2 samples of dobsonflies from EWSU (0.062 µg/g; SE = 0.0245) was 10 times greater than the sample from ESLT, and MMeHg in the composite sample of diving beetles from ESDS was more than 300 times greater than the sample from ESLT.

The one composite sample of water scavenger beetle larvae (Hydrophilidae) collected from the Elgin Mine area (ESDS) had the second highest concentration of MMeHg (0.56 µg/g) observed for either mine, and it was higher than any larval hydrophilids collected at Harley Gulch during 2007–2011 (Rytuba and others, 2011). Damselfly larvae (Coenagrionidae) had elevated concentrations of Hg_T at both ESUS (1.62 µg/g) and ESDS (0.96 µg/g), but the MMeHg concentrations, 0.142 and 0.086 µg/g, respectively, were similar to concentrations observed at the Harley Gulch reference site in 2008 (Rytuba and others, 2011). The resulting percentages of MMeHg for those two sites were consistently low, 8.8 percent and 8.9 percent for ESUS and ESDS, respectively. Damselfly larvae from the Elgin Mine area had concentrations of Hg_T and MMeHg that were similar to those found in the wetlands of Harley Gulch, where the concentration of Hg_T ranged from 0.46 to 9.94 µg/g, the MMeHg concentration ranged from 0.02 to 0.23 µg/g, and the percent MMeHg ranged from 2.29 to 4.56 percent (Rytuba and others, 2011).

Conclusions

This report evaluates the potential Hg contamination of Sulphur Creek by two historical mines, one a mercury mine (Elgin Mine) and the other a gold mine (Clyde Mine), located within the California Coast Range mercury mineral belt. Sampling carried out during low-flow conditions in late spring and early summer of 2010 demonstrated that concentrations of MMeHg were lower in both water and sediment in Freshwater Branch near the Clyde Mine than near the Elgin Mine. This could indicate that available concentrations of DOC and Hg were insufficient to produce significant amounts of MMeHg in the Freshwater Branch.

Data from the West Fork of Sulphur Creek near the Elgin Mine showed elevated Hg_T, Hg_F, and MMeHg levels in water and sediment. Concentrations of Hg ranged from 32 to 175 times higher at the Elgin Mine sample sites than at the Clyde Mine sites in filtered water (Hg_F). In unfiltered water, Hg_T ranged between 16 and 629 times higher at the Elgin Mine sample sites. The differences between MMeHg in water at the two mine sites were less extreme, ranging from 1.3 to 13 times higher at Elgin Mine sample sites than the Clyde Mine sites. Hg concentrations in sediment were 2–150 times higher at Elgin Mine sites than Clyde Mine sites, while MMeHg concentrations in sediment were 1.3–59 times higher at Elgin Mine sites than Clyde Mine sites.

With the exception of one sample of larval dobsonflies, there were no apparent trends toward increasing concentrations of Hg_T or MMeHg in biota collected in the Freshwater Branch. The elevated concentrations in the dobsonflies appeared to be an outlier and did not indicate a trend toward increased Hg bioaccumulation downstream from the mine.

Changes in Hg_T and Hg_F concentrations in water collected from the West Fork of Sulphur Creek near the Elgin Mine were relatively consistent as they progressed downstream, increasing from 10EL3 to 10EL1, and then decreasing downstream to 10EL2. Hg_F concentrations were 70–79 percent lower than Hg_T concentrations at corresponding sample sites. MMeHg in water, however, was highest at the upstream site and appeared to decline in a downstream direction, with the concentration just below the mine site the lowest of the three sampled, and the concentration at the lowest site in between the two.

Unlike the trend observed for water, concentrations of both Hg_T and MMeHg in sediment were considerably higher (by a factor of 6 and 4, respectively) at the site just downstream from the Elgin Mine than at the upstream site. Concentrations of both Hg_T and MMeHg at the site furthest downstream were lower than upstream from the mine. Sulfate concentrations were 20–40 times higher at Elgin Mine than at Clyde Mine. Concentrations of MMeHg in water and sediment at Elgin Mine were higher than at the Clyde Mine, where dissolved organic carbon (DOC) and Hg_T concentrations were likely limiting MMeHg formation.

Despite the close proximity of the two mines, few invertebrates of the same taxon were collected in both subwatersheds, making inter-watershed comparisons difficult. Three composite samples of water striders collected from each mine area indicated no significant differences between sites for either Hg_T or MMeHg. Larval dobsonflies were collected from two upper-watershed sites at Elgin Mine and three downstream Clyde Mine sites, and the concentrations of both MMeHg and Hg_T were greater at Clyde Mine sites than at Elgin Mine sites. Larval damselflies, larval water scavenger beetles, and adult predaceous diving beetles were collected only from the West Fork of Sulphur Creek (Elgin Mine), and their concentrations of Hg_T and MMeHg were higher compared with the other collected taxa. Larval dragonflies (families Gomphidae, Libellulidae, Aeshnidae, and Cordulegastridae) were collected only from Freshwater Branch (Clyde Mine), and an analysis of their concentrations of Hg_T and MMeHg revealed no significant trends.

The presence of relatively low to moderate concentrations of Hg and MMeHg in water, sediment, and biota in the Freshwater Branch, and the lack of significant increases in concentrations downstream from the mine wastes indicated that the Clyde Mine is not a significant source of Hg to the watershed during low-flow conditions. This conclusion is in accordance with previous research on this section of the Sulphur Creek watershed (Churchill and Clinkenbeard, 2003).

Streamflow in Freshwater Branch was dominated by meteoric water, in contrast with West Fork Sulphur Creek, where high-salinity thermal spring effluent represented a significant component of creek water. The conductivity of this hot-spring source was about 20–30 times higher than meteoric waters present near the Clyde Mine. This hot-spring effluent is likely a natural source of Hg to the watershed because the thermal water formation is likely related to the mineralization. The West Fork also contained elevated levels of Hg, MMeHg, and other geochemical constituents before interacting with mine-waste material. It is possible, therefore, that natural sources contribute significantly more Hg to the West Fork of Sulphur Creek than does mine-waste material from the Elgin Mine.

References Cited

Alpers, C.N., Hunerlach, M.P., May, J.T., Hothem, R.L., Taylor, H.E., Antweiler, R.C., DeWild, J.F., and Lawler, D.A., 2005, Geochemical characterization of water, sediment, and biota affected by mercury contamination and acidic drainage from historical Au mining, Greenhorn Creek, Nevada County, California, 1999–2001: U.S. Geological Survey Scientific Investigations Report 2004–5251, 278 p. (*http://pubs.usgs.gov/sir/2004/5251/*).

Bloom, N.S., 1989, Determination of picogram levels of methylmercury by aqueous phase ethylation, followed by cryogenic gas chromatography with cold vapour atomic fluorescence detection: Canadian Journal of Fisheries and Aquatic Sciences, v. 46, p. 1131–1140.

Bloom, N. S., 1992, On the chemical form of mercury in edible fish and marine invertebrate tissue. Canadian Journal of Fisheries and Aquatic Sciences, v. 49, p. 1010–1017.

Bloom, N.S., 1995, Mercury as a case study of ultra-clean sample handling and storage in aquatic trace metal research: Environmental Laboratory, v. 3–4, p. 20–25.

Bloom, N.S., Crecelius, E.A., and Fitzgerald, W.F., 1988, Determination of volatile mercury species at the picogram level by low temperature gas chromatography with cold vapor atomic fluorescence detection: Analytica Chimica Acta, v. 208, p. 151–161.

Cain, D.J., Luoma, S.N., Carter, J.L., and Fend, S.V., 1992, Aquatic insects as bioindicators of trace element contamination in cobble-bottom rivers and streams: Canadian Journal of Fisheries and Aquatic Sciences, v. 10, p. 2141–2154.

Churchill, R., and Clinkenbeard, J., 2003, Assessment of the feasibility of remediation of mercury mine sources in the Cache Creek watershed. CALFED final report. Available at: http://loer.tamug.tamu.edu/calfed/FinalReports.htm

Crock, J.G., 1996, Mercury: Chapter 29 *in* Sparks, D.L., ed., Methods of soil analysis, part 3, chemical methods: Soil Science Society of America Book Series, Number 5, p. 769–791.

Drott, A., Lambertsson, L., Björn, E., and Skyllberg, U., 2008, Do potential methylation rates reflect accumulated methyl mercury in contaminated sediments?: Environmental Science & Technology, v. 42, p.153–158.

Fishman, M.J. and Pyen, G., 1979, Determination of selected anions in water by ion chromatography: U.S. Geological Survey Water Resources Investigations 79–101, 30 p.

Gibs, J., Wilde, F.D., and Heckathorn, H.A., 2007, Use of multiparameter instruments for routine field measurements (ver. 1.1): U.S. Geological Survey Techniques of Water-Resources Investigations, book 9, chap. A6, section 6.8, August, accessed November 23, 2012 from http://pubs.water.usgs.gov/twri9A/.

Gill, G.A., and Fitzgerald, W.F., 1987, Picomolar mercury measurements in seawater and other materials using stannous chloride reduction and two-stage Au amalgamation with gas phase detection: Marine Chemistry, v. 20, p. 227–243.

Horvat, M., Bloom, N.S., and Liang, L., 1993, Comparison of distillation with other current isolation methods for the determination of methyl mercury compounds in low level environmental samples Part 1 Sediments: Analytica Chimica Acta, v. 281, p. 135–152.

Huguenin, E., 1917, Unpublished property report on the Elgin Mine, Colusa County, California: Division of Mines and Geology property files, 2 p.

Merritt, R.W., and Cummins, K.W., 1995, An introduction to the aquatic insects of North America (2nd ed.): Dubuque, Iowa, Kendall/Hunt, 862 p.

Mining and Scientific Press, 1875, Colusa County quicksilver mines: Mining and Scientific Press, v. 30, No. 6, p. 82.

National Research Council of Canada Institute for National Measurement Standards, 1999, DORM-2, DOLT-2, Dogfish muscle and liver certified reference materials for trace metals: INMS Certified Reference Materials Data Sheet, 4 p. [http://www.ems.nrc.ca/ems1.htm, last accessed January 28, 2009].

O'Leary, R.M., Hageman, P.L., and Crock, J.G., 1996, Determination of mercury in water, geologic, and plant materials by continuous flow-cold vapor-atomic absorption spectrophotometry, *in* Arbogast, B.F., ed., Quality assurance manual for the branch of geochemistry: United States Geological Survey: United States Geological Survey Open-File Report 96-525, p. 42–55.

Orion Research, Inc., 1978, Analytical methods guide (9th ed.): Cambridge, Mass., 48 p.

Rytuba, J.J., 2000, Mercury mine drainage and processes that control its environmental impact: The Science of the Total Environment, v. 260, p. 57–71.

Rytuba, J.J., R.L. Hothem, B.E. Brussee, and D.N. Goldstein, 2011, Impact of mine and natural sources of mercury on water, sediment, and biota in Harley Gulch adjacent to the Abbott-Turkey Run Mine, Lake County, California: U.S. Geological Survey Open-File Report 2011-1265, 105 p.

Tetra Tech EM Inc., 2003, Final Engineering evaluation and cost analysis for the Sulphur Creek Mining District, Colusa and Lake Counties, California. CALFED Cache Creek Study Task 5C2: Final Report, 240 p.

U.S. Bureau of Mines, 1965, Mercury potential of the United States: U.S. Department of the Interior, Bureau of Mines, Information Circular 8252, 376 p.

U.S. Environmental Protection Agency, 2001, Appendix to Method 1631 Total mercury in tissue, sludge, sediment, and soil by acid digestion and BrCl oxidation, EPA-821-R-01-013, Office of Water, Washington, DC, 13 p.

U.S. Environmental Protection Agency, 2002, Method 1631, Revision E: Mercury in water by oxidation, purge and trap, and cold vapor atomic fluorescence spectrometry, EPA-821-R-02-019, Office of Water, Washington, DC, 38 p.

U.S. Geological Survey, 2006, Collection of water samples (ver. 2.0): U.S. Geological Survey Techniques of Water-Resources Investigations, book 9, chap. A4, September 2006, accessed November 23, 2012, at http://pubs.water.usgs.gov/twri9A4/.

Watts, W.L., 1893, Colusa County, Eleventh Report of the State Mineralogist, California State Mining Bureau, Sacramento, Calif., pp. 183–184.

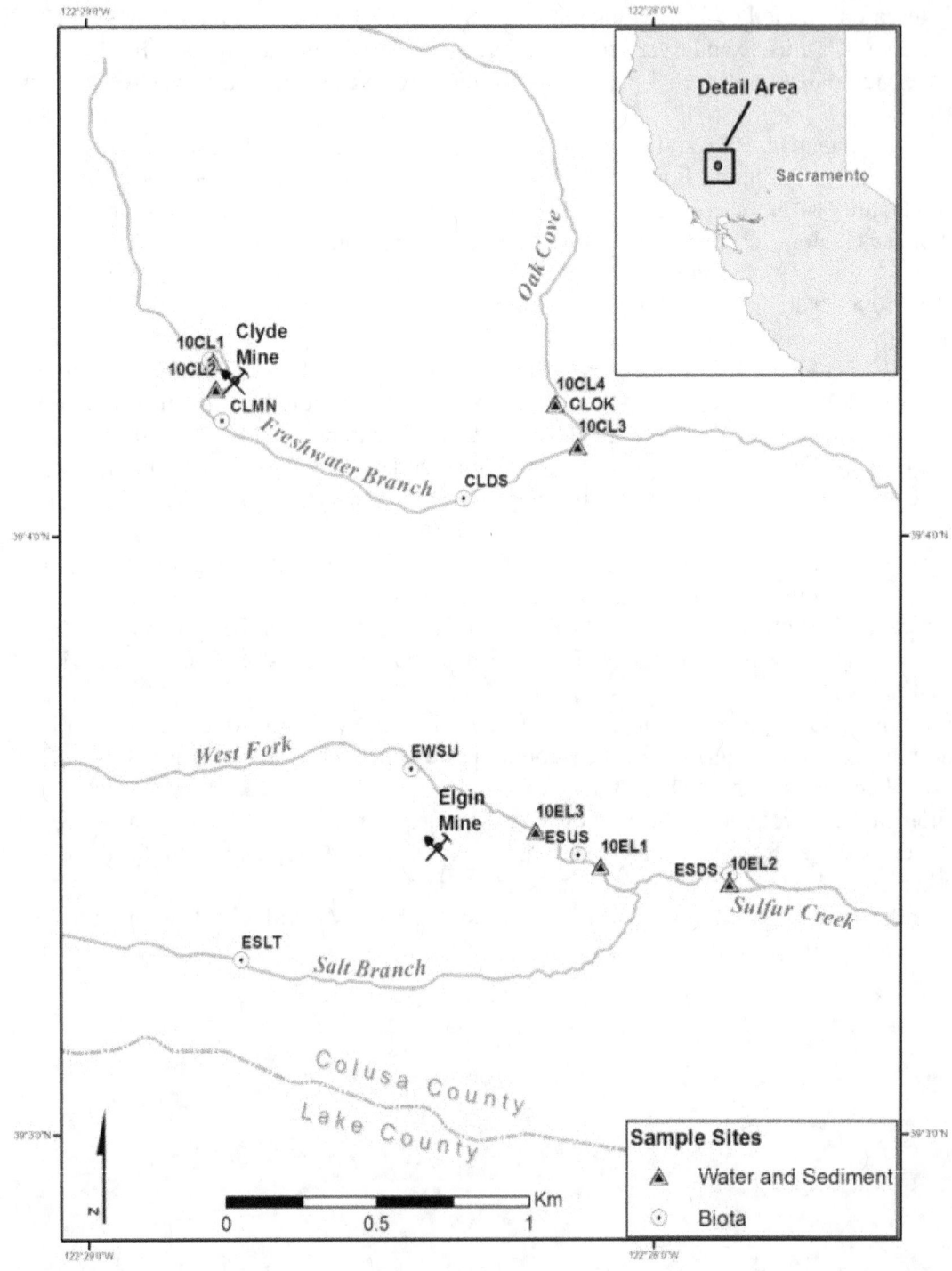

Figure 1. Study sites sampled in 2010 in the Clyde Gold Mine area and the Elgin Mercury Mine area in the headwaters of Sulphur Creek, California.

Figure 2. Clyde Mine sample site 10CL1, just downstream from biota site CLUS (see fig. 1). Photo by James Rytuba, USGS.

Figure 3. Clyde Mine sample site 10CL2, 130 meters upstream from biota site CLMN, below the main surface disruption of Clyde Mine (see fig. 1). Photo by James Rytuba, USGS.

18

Figure 4. Biota site CLDS, 380 meters upstream from water and sediment sample site 10CL3 (see fig. 1). Photo by Roger Hothem, USGS.

19

Figure 5. Biota sample site CLOK near water and sediment sample site 10CL4 (see fig. 1). Photo by Brianne Brussee, USGS.

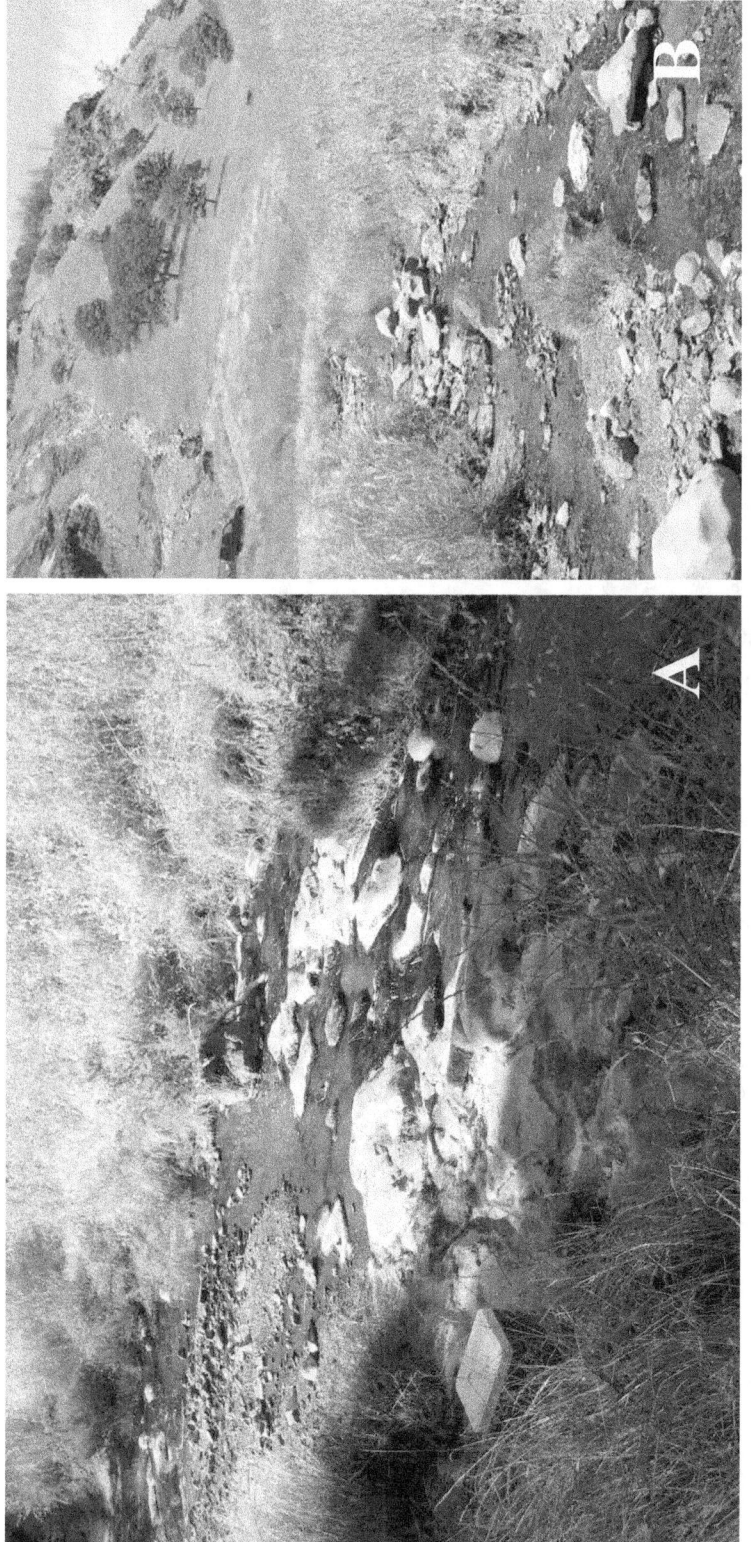

Figure 6. Water and sediment sample site 10EL1 (A) and nearby biota sample site ESUS (B) on the West Fork of Sulphur Creek, Elgin Mine area, 2010 (see table 1 and fig. 1). Photos by James Rytuba (A) and Roger Hothem (B), USGS.

Figure 7. Water and sediment sample site 10EL2 (A) and nearby biota sample site ESDS (B) on the West Fork of Sulphur Creek, Elgin Mine area, 2010 (see table 1 and fig. 3). Photos by James Rytuba (A) and Roger Hothem (B), USGS.

Figure 8. Water and sediment sample site 10EL3 (A), located about 200 meters (m) upstream from 10EL1 and upstream from input from the Elgin Mine. Photo by James Rytuba, USGS. The comparable biota site, EWSU (B), is located upstream from the Elgin Mine input and 400 m upstream from 10EL3 (see table 1 and fig. 1). Photo by Roger Hothem, USGS.

Figure 9. Biota sample site ESLT looking upstream at Salt Branch, Elgin Mine area, 2010 (see table 1 and fig. 1). Photo by Roger Hothem, USGS.

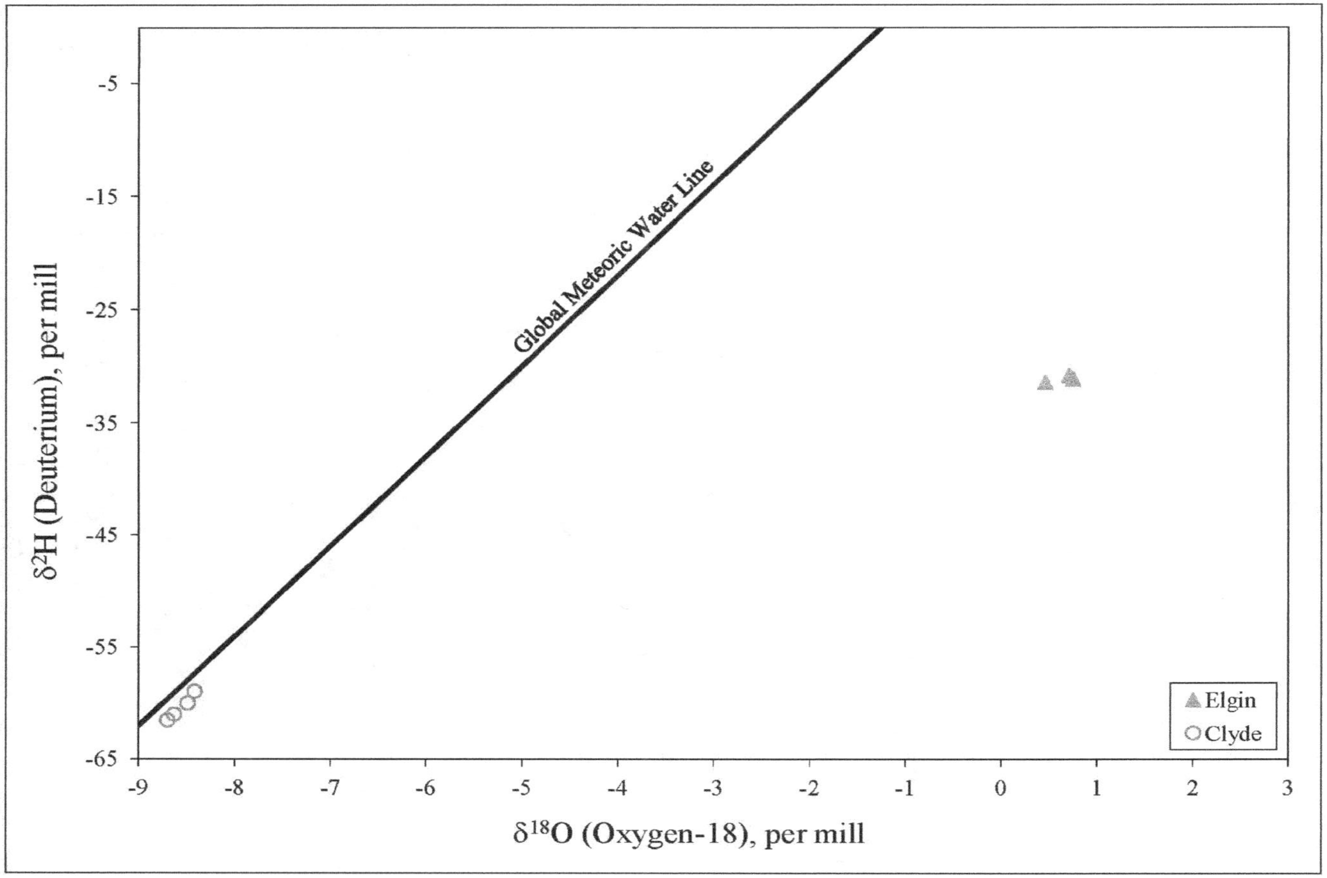

Figure 10. Plot showing oxygen and deuterium stable isotope levels in Clyde Mine and Elgin Mine water samples.

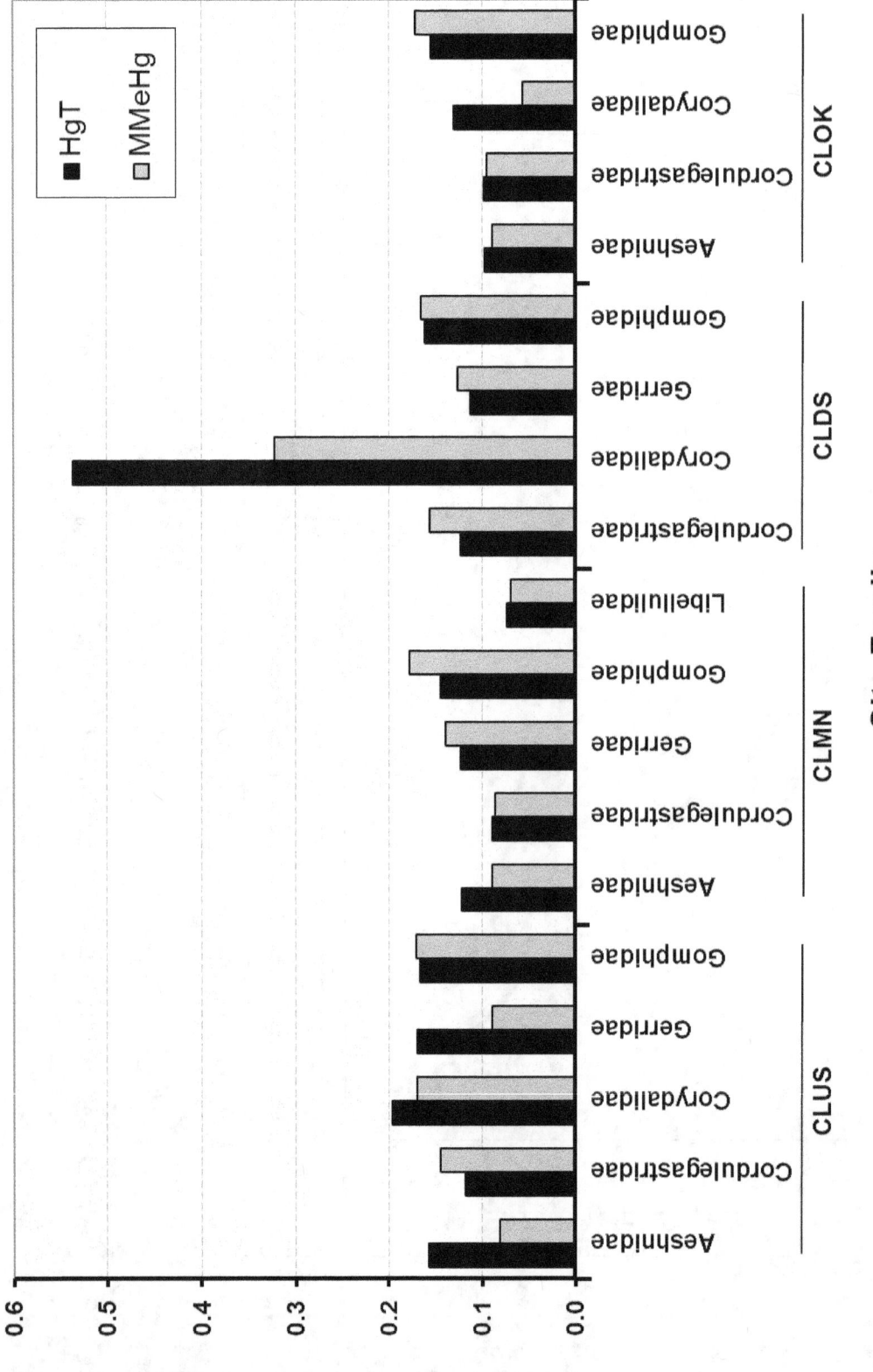

Figure 11. Total mercury (Hg$_T$) and monomethyl mercury (MMeHg) concentrations (µg/g ww) in invertebrate samples collected from Clyde Mine on April 29, 2010.

26

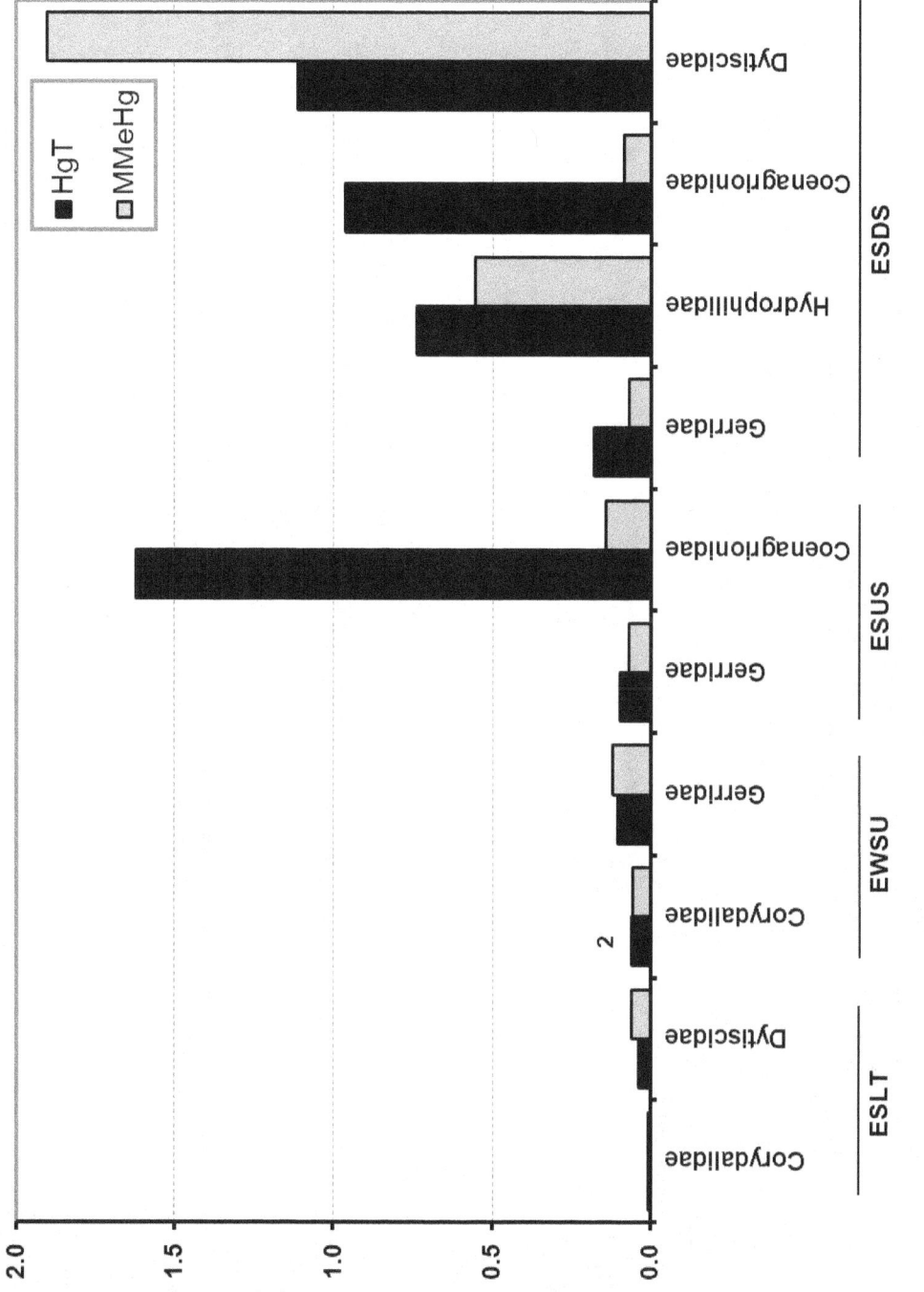

Figure 12. Total mercury (Hg$_T$) and monomethyl mercury (MMeHg) concentrations (µg/g ww) in invertebrate samples collected from Elgin Mine on May 12, 2010.

27

Table 1. Sample locations for water, sediment, and biota for the Clyde Gold Mine and Elgin Mercury Mine, 2010.

[°, degrees; ', minutes; ", seconds]

Site description	Biota				Water and sediment			
	Site name	Sampling date	Latitude	Longitude	Site name	Sampling date	Latitude	Longitude
CLYDE MINE								
Freshwater Branch upstream Clyde Mine	CLUS	4/29/2010	39° 04' 17.7"	122° 28' 47.1"	10CL1	7/2/2010	39° 04' 17.5"	122° 28' 46.7"
Freshwater Branch at Clyde Mine	CLMN	4/29/2010	39° 04' 11.6"	122° 28' 45.8"	10CL2	7/2/2010	39° 04' 14.8"	122° 28' 46.4"
Freshwater Branch downstream Clyde Mine	CLDS	4/29/2010	39° 04' 03.8"	122° 28' 20.0"	10CL3	7/2/2010	39° 04' 09.0"	122° 28' 08.0"
Oak Cove tributary to Freshwater Branch	CLOK	4/29/2010	39° 04' 13.2"	122° 28' 10.1"	10CL4	7/2/2010	39° 04' 13.3"	122° 28' 10.3"
ELGIN MINE								
Salt Branch upstream from road	ESLT	5/13/2010	39° 03' 17.5"	122° 28' 43.9"	Not sampled			
West Fork Sulfur Creek upstream Elgin Mine	EWSU	5/13/2010	39° 03' 36.6"	122° 28' 25.7"	Not sampled			
West Fork Sulphur Creek upstream Elgin Mine tailings pile	Not sampled				10EL3	6/30/2010	39° 03' 30.4"	122° 28' 12.4"
West Fork Sulphur Creek upstream Salt Branch	ESUS	5/13/2010	39° 03' 28.0"	122° 28' 08.0"	10EL1	6/30/2010	39° 03' 26.9"	122° 28' 05.6"
West Fork Sulphur Creek downstream Salt Branch	ESDS	5/13/2010	39° 03' 26.0"	122° 27' 52.0"	10EL2	6/30/2010	39° 03' 25.1"	122° 27' 52.0"

Table 2. Physical and selected chemical parameters and total mercury (Hg$_T$), monomethyl mercury (MMeHg), and dissolved organic carbon (DOC) concentrations in waters and sediment from the Clyde and Elgin mines, 2010.

[µS/cm, microsiemens per centimeter; °C, degrees Celsius; O$_2$, Oxygen; ng/L, nanograms per liter; DOC, dissolved organic carbon; mg/L, milligrams per liter]

Sample site	Sampling date	Conductivity (µS/cm)	pH	Temperature (°C)	Dissolved O$_2$ (ppm)	Water				Sediment		
						Hg$_T$ (ng/L)	Hg$_F$ (ng/L)	MMeHg (ng/L)	DOC (mg/L)	Hg$_T$ (ng/g)	MMeHg (ng/g)	MMeHg/Hg (percent)
CLYDE MINE												
10CL1A	7/2/2010	750	7.37	17.21	6.91	16.0	9.45	0.226	2.1	259	0.485	0.187
10CL2A	7/2/2010	781	7.62	17.51	7.80	76.1	7.81	0.085	2.5	188	0.068	0.036
10CL3A	7/2/2010	998	7.89	18.90	8.58	3.45	3.14	0.232	2.6	352	0.518	0.147
10CL4A	7/2/2010	730	7.82	19.21	9.33	2.51	2.25	0.101	3.0	109	0.15	0.138
ELGIN MINE												
10EL1A	6/30/2010	25129	8.50	29.78	7.00	1580	394	0.307	4.3	16400	4.04	0.025
10EL2A	6/30/2010	23097	7.57	28.98	7.57	1200	362	0.531	6.6	761	0.667	0.088
10EL3A	6/30/2010	25899	8.56	25.47	1.40	1450	305	1.11	4.1	2800	0.968	0.035

Table 3. Mercury and associated major and minor elements in sediment, precipitates, Clyde Mine, 2010.

[ppm, parts per million]

Sample site	Hg (ppm)	Ag (ppm)	Al (percent)	As (ppm)	Ba (ppm)	Be ppm	Bi (ppm)	Ca (percent)	Cd (ppm)	Ce (ppm)	Co (ppm)	Cr (ppm)	Cs (ppm)	Cu (ppm)	Fe (percent)	Ga (ppm)
10CL1S2	0.81	0.05	7.67	8.9	600	1.30	0.19	0.67	0.15	36.1	54.3	1330	4.00	53.1	6.34	18.7
10CL2S2	3.63	0.07	7.09	7.6	540	1.29	0.13	0.45	0.14	31.4	58.1	806	3.71	47.8	5.94	16.4
10CL3S2	1.41	0.07	5.99	5.8	500	1.01	0.10	0.51	0.14	26.6	66.3	960	12.9	45.1	5.73	13.6

Sample site	Ge (ppm)	Hf (ppm)	In (ppm)	K (percent)	La (ppm)	Li (ppm)	Mg (percent)	Mn (ppm)	Mo (ppm)	Na (percent)	Nb (ppm)	Ni (ppm)	P (ppm)	Pb (ppm)	Rb (ppm)	S (percent)
10CL1S2	0.23	2.5	0.066	1.52	17.5	61.0	5.74	828	0.76	0.88	7.0	658	490	13.5	66.8	0.01
10CL2S2	0.19	2.3	0.058	1.36	14.7	93.7	7.50	893	0.69	0.79	6.1	835	450	11.4	56.1	0.01
10CL3S2	0.21	1.9	0.049	1.08	11.8	59.1	8.65	977	0.62	0.79	5.2	994	410	9.40	46.0	0.02

Sample site	Sb (ppm)	Sc (ppm)	Se (ppm)	Sn (ppm)	Sr (ppm)	Ta (ppm)	Te (ppm)	Th (ppm)	Ti (percent)	Tl (ppm)	U (ppm)	V (ppm)	W (ppm)	Y (ppm)	Zn (ppm)	Zr (ppm)
10CL1S2	2.56	20.9	2	1.6	84.1	0.50	0.09	5.5	0.359	0.46	1.6	171	1.8	15.8	131	75.2
10CL2S2	5.62	19.1	1	1.3	72.8	0.43	0.08	4.9	0.328	0.61	1.4	154	1.3	13.3	111	70.5
10CL3S2	2.75	17.1	1	1.1	66.1	0.37	0.07	3.9	0.305	0.36	1.1	132	2.5	12.4	102	58.9

30

Table 4. Mercury and associated major and minor elements in sediment, precipitates, Elgin Mine. 2010.

[ppm, parts per million]

Sample site	Hg (ppm)	Ag (ppm)	Al (percent)	As (ppm)	Ba (ppm)	Be (ppm)	Bi (ppm)	Ca (ppm)	Cd (ppm)	Ce (ppm)	Co (ppm)	Cr (ppm)	Cs (ppm)	Cu (ppm)	Fe (percent)	Ga (ppm)
10EL1S2	292	0.05	6.90	5.3	1850	0.85	0.08	2.62	0.15	28.2	38.2	2520	80.4	45.1	5.90	15.35
10EL2S2	130	0.06	6.80	5.6	2260	0.98	0.11	1.39	0.18	28.2	46.7	3720	61.1	46.7	6.45	16.35
10EL3S2	30.4	0.07	6.75	5.2	1440	0.96	0.09	1.37	0.32	25.2	40.1	846	72.0	44.6	6.17	15.25

Sample site	Ge (ppm)	Hf (ppm)	In (ppm)	K (percent)	La (ppm)	Li (ppm)	Mg (percent)	Mn (ppm)	Mo (ppm)	Na (percent)	Nb (ppm)	Ni (ppm)	P (ppm)	Pb (ppm)	Rb (ppm)	S (percent)
10EL1S2	0.18	2.4	0.055	1.27	13.1	79.2	4.08	836	0.68	1.81	5.1	305	590	8.0	62.0	0.11
10EL2S2	0.19	2.7	0.062	1.30	12.8	79.9	5.16	831	0.84	1.74	5.9	420	640	7.7	60.3	0.21
10EL3S2	0.16	2.5	0.058	1.32	11.7	74.5	5.23	823	0.83	2.00	5.3	436	630	7.4	59.8	0.22

Sample site	Sb (ppm)	Sc (ppm)	Se (ppm)	Sn (ppm)	Sr (ppm)	Ta (ppm)	Te (ppm)	Th (ppm)	Ti (percent)	Tl (ppm)	U (ppm)	V (ppm)	W (ppm)	Y (ppm)	Zn (ppm)	Zr (ppm)
10EL1S2	0.89	20.5	1	1.9	529	0.36	0.08	3.0	0.476	0.27	1.0	183	10.3	17.5	117	73.7
10EL2S2	1.22	22.0	1	1.2	207	0.42	0.08	3.4	0.507	0.33	1.1	197	15.7	19.0	128	81.8
10EL3S2	1.16	20.5	2	1.2	196	0.38	0.07	3.2	0.506	0.32	1.0	189	14.4	17.3	113	76.0

Table 5. Concentration of anions and selected cations in filtered water at the Clyde and Elgin mines, 2010.

[ppm, parts per million; mg/L, milligrams per liter; µg/L, micrograms per liter; <, less than]

Sample site	Cl (ppm)	F (ppm)	NO₃ (ppm)	SO₄ (ppm)	CaCO₃ (ppm)	Ca (mg/L)	Fe (µg/L)	K (mg/L)	Li (µg/L)	Mg (mg/L)	Na (mg/L)
CLYDE MINE											
10CL1C	10.2	<0.04	<0.08	22.4	418.0	24.2	NA	0.678	36.0	82.8	5.20
10CL2C	10.3	<0.04	<0.08	23.0	438.5	24.9	NA	0.746	56.7	86.7	5.15
10CL3C	18.9	<0.04	<0.08	11.4	583.5	19.6	NA	0.703	47.8	118	13.8
10CL4C	10.0	<0.04	<0.08	12.0	416.5	25.6	NA	0.575	17.0	78.4	6.17
ELGIN MINE											
10EL1C	8379	14.9	398	441.0	3082.4	21.3	71.1	307	7390	69.3	5120
10EL2C	8090	15.1	406	468.8	2765.5	25.0	39.1	283	6560	69.7	4770
10EL3C	8394	14.8	348	439.1	3380.3	22.8	85.0	326	7270	71.3	5750

32

Table 6. Concentrations of relevant geochemical constituents in samples of filtered water from the Freshwater Branch of Sulphur Creek adjacent to the Clyde Mine.

[µg/L, micrograms per liter; mg/L, milligrams per liter; <, less than]

Sample site	B (µg/L)	Ba (µg/L)	Ca (mg/L)	Cs (µg/L)	K (mg/L)	Li (µg/L)	Mg (mg/L)	Na (mg/L)	Ni (µg/L)	Rb (µg/L)	SiO₂ (mg/L)	Sr (µg/L)	W (µg/L)	Y (µg/L)
10CL1B	108	56.4	24.2	< 0.2	0.678	36.0	82.8	5.20	4.8	0.30	74.3	395	5.3	0.12
10CL2B	95.4	85.1	24.9	< 0.2	0.746	56.7	86.7	5.15	5.4	0.22	70.5	475	< 5	0.10
10CL3B	574	64.3	19.6	0.58	0.703	47.8	118	13.8	5.5	0.86	76.5	382	7.53	0.15
10CL4B	179	39.2	25.6	< 0.2	0.575	17.0	78.4	6.17	< 4	0.20	68.8	290	< 5	0.14

Not detected (in µg/L) : Ag <10, Al <20, As <10, Be <0.5, Bi <2, Cd <0.2, Ce <0.1, Co <0.2, Cr <10, Cu <5, Dy <0.05, Er <0.05, Eu <0.05, Fe <500, Ga <0.5, Gd <0.05, Ge<0.5, Ho <0.05, La <0.1, Lu <0.1, Mn <1, Mo <20, Nb <2, Nd <2, Ni <0.1, P<0.1, Pb <0.5, Pr <0.1, Sb <0.1, Sc <6, Se <10, Sm <0.1, SO₄ <20, Ta <0.2, Tb <0.05, Th <2, Ti <5, Tl <1, Tm <0.05, U <1, V <5, Yb <0.05, Zn <5, Zr <2

33

Table 7. Concentrations of relevant geochemical constituents in samples of unfiltered water from the Freshwater Branch of Sulphur Creek adjacent to the Clyde Mine, 2010.

[µg/L, micrograms per liter; mg/L, milligrams per liter; <, less than]

Sample site	Al (µg/L)	B (µg/L)	Ba (µg/L)	Ca (mg/L)	Ce (µg/L)	Co (µg/L)	Cs (µg/L)	Dy (µg/L)	Fe (µg/L)	Ge (µg/L)	K (mg/L)	Li (µg/L)
10CL1A	20.7	110	55.2	24.3	<0.1	<0.2	<0.2	<0.05	<20	<0.5	<0.3	14.7
10CL2A	926	82.3	89.3	25.4	0.62	1.4	<0.2	0.071	1710	<0.5	0.3	41.4
10CL3A	25.8	565	63.8	20	<0.1	0.33	0.6	<0.05	37.2	<0.5	0.42	17.6
10CL4A	<20	150	40.9	25.4	<0.1	<0.2	<0.2	0.057	<20	<0.5	<0.3	<1

Sample site	Mg (mg/L)	Mn (µg/L)	Na (mg/L)	Nd (µg/L)	Ni (µg/L)	Rb (µg/L)	SiO$_2$ (mg/L)	Sr (µg/L)	W (µg/L)	Y (µg/L)	Zn (µg/L)
10CL1A	80.2	<2	5.00	<0.1	6.40	0.30	74.6	385	5.05	0.12	<5
10CL2A	86.6	46	4.84	0.24	24.5	0.86	74.3	467	<5	0.24	6.2
10CL3A	117	<2	13.8	<0.1	9.80	0.80	78.2	367	6.85	0.16	<5
10CL4A	76.7	<2	5.87	0.18	<4	0.21	67.3	283	<5	0.23	<5

Not detected (in µg/L): Ag <10, As <10, Be <0.5, Bi <2, Cd <0.2, Cr <10, Cu <5, Er <0.05, Eu <0.05, Ga <0.5, Gd < 0.05, Ho <0.05, La <0.1, Lu <1, Mo <20, Nb <2, P<0.1 m, Pb <0.5, Pr <0.1, Sb <3, Sc <3, Sc <6, Se <10, Sm <0.1, SO$_4$ <20, Ta <0.2, Tb <0.05, Th <2, Tl <1, Tm <0.05, U <1, V <5, Yb <0.05, Zr <2

34

Table 8. Concentrations of relevant geochemical constituents in samples of filtered water from the West Fork of Sulphur Creek near the Elgin Mine, 2010.

[μg/L, micrograms per liter; mg/L, milligrams per liter; <, less than]

Sample site	Al (μg/L)	As (μg/L)	B (mg/L)	Ba (μg/L)	Ca (mg/L)	Ce (μg/L)	Co (μg/L)	Cs (μg/L)	Dy (μg/L)	Eu (μg/L)	Fe (μg/L)	Gd (μg/L)
10EL1B	27.2	32.2	157	1160	21.3	0.27	2.13	617	0.080	0.052	71.1	0.057
10EL2B	22.4	29.0	144	799	25.0	0.13	2.12	557	0.057	0.064	39.1	<0.05
10EL3B	21.4	29.0	151	1280	22.8	0.17	1.85	626	0.098	0.066	85.0	0.089

Sample site	Ge (μg/L)	K (mg/L)	Li (μg/L)	Mg (mg/L)	Mn (μg/L)	Na (mg/L)	Nd (μg/L)	Ni (μg/L)	P (mg/L)	Pb (μg/L)	Rb (μg/L)	Sb (μg/L)
10EL1B	24.7	307	6700	69.3	50.6	5120	0.23	30.0	0.1	0.57	970	6.23
10EL2B	20.2	283	6300	69.7	15.3	4770	<0.1	27.0	0.1	<0.5	895	5.65
10EL3B	26.3	326	6940	71.3	66.2	5750	0.18	29.4	0.1	<0.5	1010	6.30

Sample site	Sc (μg/L)	Se (μg/L)	SiO$_2$ (mg/L)	Sr (μg/L)	Ti (μg/L)	V (μg/L)	W (μg/L)	Y (μg/L)	Yb (μg/L)	Zn (μg/L)
10EL1B	6.7	100	77.6	1140	6.5	6.1	1610	0.62	<0.05	8.4
10EL2B	5.9	96	72.0	1360	7.0	7.1	1530	0.30	<0.05	<5
10EL3B	6.5	108	80.5	1240	7.0	5.6	1720	0.52	0.07	<5

Not detected (in μg/L): Ag <10, Be <0.5, Bi <2, Cd <0.2, Cr <10, Cu <5, Er <0.05, Ga <0.5, Ho <0.05, La <0.1, Lu <1, Mo <20, Nb <2, Pr <0.1, Sm <0.1, Ta <0.2, Tb <0.05, Th <2, Tl <1, Tm <0.05, U <1, Zr <2

Table 9. Concentrations of relevant geochemical constituents in samples of unfiltered water from the West Fork of Sulphur Creek near the Elgin Mine, 2010.

[µg/L, micrograms per liter; mg/L, milligrams per liter; <, less than]

Sample site	Al (µg/L)	As (µg/L)	B (mg/L)	Ba (µg/L)	Ca (mg/L)	Cd (µg/L)	Ce (µg/L)	Co (µg/L)	Cs (µg/L)	Dy (µg/L)	Er (µg/L)	Eu (µg/L)	Fe (µg/L)
10EL1A	465	32.6	137	1270	21.2	<0.2	0.62	2.90	637	0.180	0.093	0.094	997
10EL2A	289	29.1	138	843	26.5	<0.2	0.36	2.36	566	0.075	0.056	<0.05	554
10EL3A	483	32.8	164	1320	24.2	0.32	0.54	2.41	623	0.200	0.100	<0.05	905

Sample site	Gd (µg/L)	Ge (µg/L)	K (mg/L)	La (µg/L)	Li (µg/L)	Mg (mg/L)	Mn (µg/L)	Na (mg/L)	Nd (µg/L)	Ni (µg/L)	P (mg/L)	Rb (µg/L)	Sb (µg/L)
10EL1A	0.160	27.9	298	0.19	6880	80.7	71.8	4900	0.62	43.6	0.2	1010	7.37
10EL2A	0.095	20.8	293	0.29	6440	79.3	27.7	5240	0.21	34.8	0.2	910	6.19
10EL3A	0.130	27.0	333	0.16	7170	79.3	84.0	5470	0.57	41.5	0.1	1020	7.00

Sample site	Sc (µg/L)	Se (µg/L)	SiO_2 (mg/L)	Sm (µg/L)	Sr (µg/L)	Ti (µg/L)	V (µg/L)	W (µg/L)	Y (µg/L)	Zn (µg/L)
10EL1A	8	102	72.3	0.23	1200	13.3	7.7	1480	1.06	15.3
10EL2A	7	94.4	77.2	<0.1	1410	10.9	7.8	1510	0.60	8.2
10EL3A	8	102	84.3	0.12	1280	9.2	6.1	1570	1.02	10.9

Not detected (in µg/L): Ag <10, Be <0.5, Bi <2, Cd <0.2, Cr <10, Cu <5, Ga <0.5, Ho <0.05, Lu <1, Mo <20, Nb <2, Pr <0.1, Sm <0.1, Ta <0.2, Tb <0.05, Th <2, Tl <1, Tm <0.05, U <1, Zr <2

Table 10. Total mercury (Hg$_T$) and monomethyl mercury (MMeHg) concentrations (µg/g ww) in biota collected from the Clyde and Elgin mines, 2010.

[ave., average; g, grams; µg/g, micrograms per gram; ww, wet weight; NA, not analyzed]

Site code	Common name	Order	Family	Number	Mass (g)	Ave. mass (g)	Hg$_T$ (µg/g)	MMeHg (µg/g)	MMeHg (percent)	Moisture (percent)
CLYDE MINE										
CLOK	Dragonfly larvae	Odonata	Gomphidae	4	1.21	0.30	0.155	0.171	110.3	76.8
CLOK	Dragonfly larvae	Odonata	Aeshnidae	8	3.57	0.45	0.098	0.089	91.1	82.4
CLOK	Dragonfly larvae	Odonata	Cordulegastridae	1	0.93	0.93	0.098	0.096	97.5	73.5
CLOK	Dobsonfly larvae	Megaloptera	Corydalidae	2	0.65	0.33	0.131	0.057	43.4	NA
CLUS	Dobsonfly larvae	Megaloptera	Corydalidae	2	1.15	0.58	0.196	0.169	86.2	77.4
CLUS	Water strider adults	Hemiptera	Gerridae	11	0.72	0.07	0.169	0.089	52.6	NA
CLUS	Dragonfly larvae	Odonata	Aeshnidae	4	2.16	0.54	0.157	0.081	51.7	77.7
CLUS	Dragonfly larvae	Odonata	Gomphidae	2	0.62	0.31	0.166	0.170	102.4	NA
CLUS	Dragonfly larvae	Odonata	Cordulegastridae	2	2.80	1.40	0.118	0.144	122.0	76.2
CLMN	Dragonfly larvae	Odonata	Aeshnidae	6	3.37	0.56	0.122	0.090	73.4	76.2
CLMN	Water strider adults	Hemiptera	Gerridae	23	1.72	0.07	0.123	0.139	113.0	65.0
CLMN	Dragonfly larvae	Odonata	Libellulidae	9	1.73	0.19	0.074	0.070	94.3	84.2
CLMN	Dragonfly larvae	Odonata	Cordulegastridae	1	1.44	1.44	0.090	0.086	96.0	74.6
CLMN	Dragonfly larvae	Odonata	Gomphidae	2	0.60	0.30	0.144	0.177	122.9	NA
CLDS	Dragonfly larvae	Odonata	Gomphidae	2	0.51	0.26	0.161	0.165	102.5	NA
CLDS	Dragonfly larvae	Odonata	Cordulegastridae	3	2.48	0.83	0.123	0.156	126.8	71.9
CLDS	Dobsonfly larvae	Megaloptera	Corydalidae	2	0.38	0.19	0.536	0.323	60.3	NA
CLDS	Water strider adults	Hemiptera	Gerridae	15	1.07	0.07	0.113	0.127	112.4	NA
ELGIN MINE										
ESDS	Water strider adults	Hemiptera	Gerridae	21	1.45	0.069	0.180	0.068	38.0	81.2
ESDS	Damselfly larvae	Odonata	Coenagrionidae	30	1.65	0.055	0.962	0.086	8.9	NA
ESDS	Water scavenger beetle larvae	Coleoptera	Hydrophilidae	11	1.14	0.104	0.737	0.556	75.4	NA
ESDS	Predaceous diving beetle adults	Coleoptera	Dytiscidae	11	0.66	0.060	1.110	1.900	171.2	60
ESUS	Water strider adults	Hemiptera	Gerridae	13	0.86	0.066	0.099	0.068	69.1	NA
ESUS	Damselfly larvae	Odonata	Coenagrionidae	12	0.55	0.046	1.620	0.142	8.8	NA
EWSU	Dobsonfly larvae	Megaloptera	Corydalidae	5	1.17	0.234	0.051	0.037	72.0	60.8
EWSU	Dobsonfly larvae	Megaloptera	Corydalidae	1	1.02	1.020	0.073	0.086	118.6	NA
EWSU	Water strider adults	Hemiptera	Gerridae	6	0.39	0.065	0.103	0.118	114.6	NA
ESLT	Predaceous diving beetle adults	Coleoptera	Dytiscidae	35	1.79	0.051	0.038	0.059	155.1	NA
ESLT	Dobsonfly larvae	Megaloptera	Corydalidae	2	1.16	0.580	0.008	0.006	72.7	NA

www.ingramcontent.com/pod-product-compliance
Lightning Source LLC
Chambersburg PA
CBHW080345290526
45791CB00009BA/2740